SUPER SIMPLE
ENGINEERING PROJECTS

ENGINEER IT!

ROAD

PROJECTS

CAROLYN BERNHARDT

CONSULTING EDITOR, DIANE CRAIG, M.A./READING SPECIALIST

Super Sandcastle

An Imprint of Abdo Publishing
abdopublishing.com

abdopublishing.com

Published by Abdo Publishing, a division of ABDO, PO Box 398166, Minneapolis, Minnesota 55439. Copyright © 2018 by Abdo Consulting Group, Inc. International copyrights reserved in all countries. No part of this book may be reproduced in any form without written permission from the publisher. Super SandCastle™ is a trademark and logo of Abdo Publishing.

Printed in the United States of America, North Mankato, Minnesota
062017
092017

THIS BOOK CONTAINS
RECYCLED MATERIALS

Production: Mighty Media, Inc.
Editor: Liz Salzmann
Cover Photographs: Mighty Media, Inc.; Shutterstock
Interior Photographs: Mighty Media, Inc.; Shutterstock

The following manufacturers/names appearing in this book are trademarks:
Craft Smart®, Crayola®, Nestle® Toll House®, Oreo®, Pillsbury Creamy Supreme®

Publisher's Cataloging-in-Publication Data

Names: Bernhardt, Carolyn, author.
Title: Engineer it! road projects / by Carolyn Bernhardt.
Other titles: Road projects
Description: Minneapolis, MN : Abdo Publishing, 2018. | Series: Super simple
    engineering projects
Identifiers: LCCN 2016963086 | ISBN 9781532111259 (lib. bdg.) |
    ISBN 9781680789102 (ebook)
Subjects: LCSH: Roads--Juvenile literature. | Roads--Design and construction--
    Juvenile literature. | Civil engineering--Juvenile literature.
Classification: DDC 624--dc23
LC record available at http://lccn.loc.gov/2016963086

Super SandCastle™ books are created by a team of professional educators, reading specialists, and content developers around five essential components—phonemic awareness, phonics, vocabulary, text comprehension, and fluency—to assist young readers as they develop reading skills and strategies and increase their general knowledge. All books are written, reviewed, and leveled for guided reading and early reading intervention programs for use in shared, guided, and independent reading and writing activities to support a balanced approach to literacy instruction.

TO ADULT HELPERS

The projects in this title are fun and simple. There are just a few things to remember. Some projects require the use of sharp objects. Also, kids may be using messy materials such as glue or paint. Make sure they protect their clothes and work surfaces. Review the projects before starting, and be ready to assist when necessary.

KEY SYMBOL

Watch for this warning symbol in this book. Here is what it means.

SHARP!
You will be working with a sharp object. Get help!

CONTENTS

WHAT IS A ROAD?

A road is a hard, flat surface that people travel on. Roads make it easier to move from one place to another.

About 2,000 years ago, the ancient Romans built the first large system of roads. There were Roman roads throughout Europe, Africa, and the Middle East. Then, about 600 years ago, the **Incas** built a road system in South America.

ROMAN ROAD

INCAN ROAD

MODERN ROADS

Road-building methods have changed a lot since ancient times. In the 1900s, the invention of the car led to many road improvements. Roads needed to be stronger to support the faster, heavier **traffic** of cars and trucks. Today, there are millions of miles of roads to take you wherever you want to go!

ROAD
CONSTRUCTION

oads are built in layers. First, the ground is leveled to create a roadbed. Then layers of gravel are added. Big machines roll over the gravel to pack it down. Finally, layers of either asphalt or concrete are added.

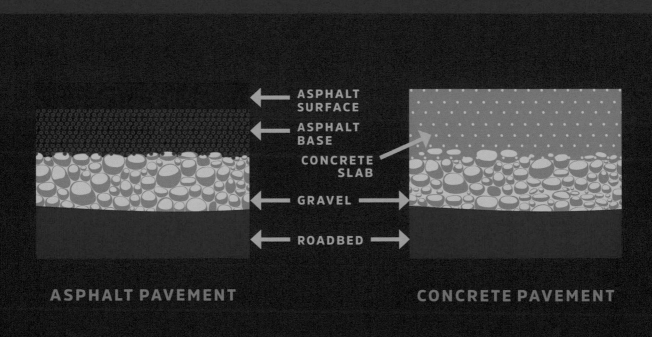

ASPHALT
SURFACE

ASPHALT
BASE

CONCRETE
SLAB

GRAVEL

ROADBED

ASPHALT PAVEMENT

CONCRETE PAVEMENT

POURING CONCRETE

Concrete is sand and gravel mixed with cement. Road workers pour concrete when it is wet. They pour the concrete into molds called forms. The forms hold the concrete in place while it dries. Special machines smooth the concrete so it dries evenly.

SPREADING ASPHALT

Asphalt is sand and gravel mixed with a black, sticky **substance** called **bitumen**. Workers heat the asphalt and spread it on the road while it's hot. Then machines roll over the asphalt to smooth it out. When the asphalt cools, it becomes a hard surface.

TYPES OF ROADS

Three main types of roads are streets, highways, and expressways.

STREET

Roads in towns are called streets. They are used to travel short distances. Streets have stop signs or stoplights to control **traffic**. Houses, apartments, and businesses are built along streets.

HIGHWAY

Highways are roads between towns. They have one or two lanes for each direction. Cars go faster on highways than on streets. Highways have few **intersections** so cars don't have to stop as often.

ROUTE 66

Route 66 was formed in 1926. It was one of the first highways in the US Highway System. Route 66 crossed eight states between Chicago, Illinois, and Santa Monica, California. By 1986, the government stopped maintaining Route 66. However, parts of it are still drivable to this day.

EXPRESSWAY

An expressway is a divided highway. Expressways have two or more lanes for each direction. There is a wall or a strip of land between the opposing lanes. Expressways have fewer curves and hills than highways. Expressways don't have any **intersections**. Instead, cars use exits to get on and off expressways. Expressways are also called freeways or superhighways.

MATERIALS

Here are some of the materials that you will need for the projects in this book.

AIR-DRY CLAY

CARDBOARD

CARDBOARD BOX

CHOCOLATE CHIPS

CRAFT FOAM

CRAFT KNIFE

CRISPY RICE CEREAL

CUTTING MAT

DUCT TAPE

FROSTING

GLASS BAKING DISH

HOLE PUNCH

LARGE NAIL

OREOS

PAINT

PAINTBRUSHES

PAPER FASTENERS

PLASTIC BAG

PLASTIC CONTAINER

PONY BEADS

RUBBER BANDS

RUBBER SPATULA

SAND

SMALL GLASS TILES

SPRINKLES

WHITE CORRECTION TAPE

WOODEN CRAFT STICKS

WOODEN SKEWERS

WOODEN SPOON

WOODEN WHEELS

ROMAN ROAD
DRAINAGE

MATERIALS: plastic container, rocks, sand, pebbles, air-dry clay, small glass tiles, water

Flooding can be a big problem on some roads. When it rains, a roadbed can fill with water and become a river. This is why it's important for roads to have a good **drainage** system. A drainage system provides a place for the water on the road to flow into.

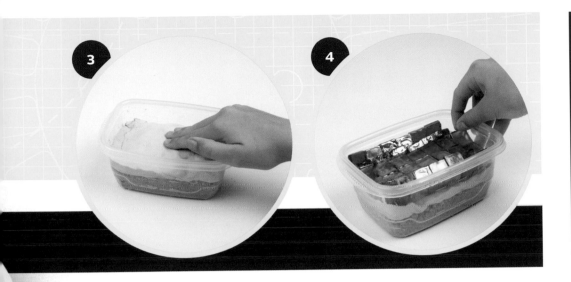

① Line the bottom of the plastic container with rocks.

② Cover the rocks with sand. Add a layer of pebbles.

③ Cover the pebbles with air-dry clay. This is the cement.

④ Press the glass tiles into the air-dry clay. Make a flat surface in the middle. Place tiles in rows that form a *V* shape on each side. The *V* shapes are **drainage ditches**.

⑤ Try sprinkling water on your road. Watch how the drainage ditches work.

ROMAN ROAD
TREAT

MATERIALS: Oreos, plastic bag, wooden spoon, glass baking dish, chocolate chips, sprinkles, crispy rice cereal, frosting, rubber spatula, Honey Grahams

Like engineers of today, the Romans built roads in layers. Similar to today's roads, the lower layers were made of dirt, crushed rock, and cement mixed with sand and gravel. Then the Romans added a layer of large, flat stones on top.

① Put Oreos in a plastic bag. Crush them with a wooden spoon. Press the **crumbs** into the bottom of the baking dish. This is the dirt layer at the bottom of the road.

② Add a layer of chocolate chips. This represents the crushed rock.

③ Mix sprinkles and crispy rice into the frosting. These are the sand, gravel, and cement.

④ Spread the cement mixture over the chocolate chips.

⑤ Press Honey Grahams in rows over the cement. These are the flat stones that complete the road.

⑥ Scoop out some Roman Road for a treat!

HIGHWAY DESIGN
PUZZLE BOARD

MATERIALS: ruler, pencil, cardboard, scissors, hole punch, black paint, paintbrush, white correction tape

Have you ever noticed the way a road twists and turns? These twists and turns are carefully **designed**. Roads need to **intersect** with each other and wind around **obstacles** to take you where you need to go.

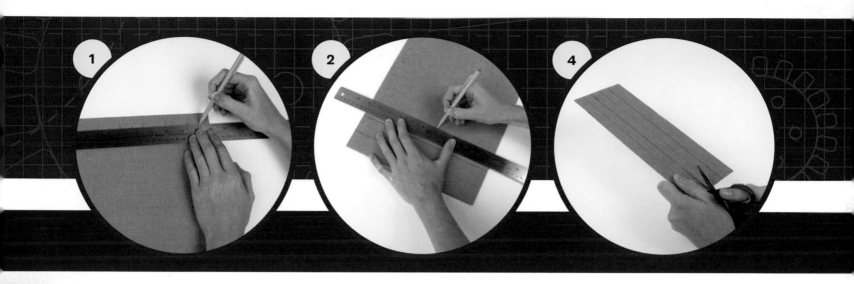

1   Make marks ¾ inches (2 cm) apart along one side of a sheet of cardboard. Repeat along the opposite side.

2   Use the ruler and pencil to draw lines connecting every other pair of marks.

3   Use the ruler and the pencil to draw lighter lines connecting the remaining pairs of marks.

4   Cut the cardboard into strips along the darker lines.

5   Cut the strips into various lengths. These are straight road pieces.

Continued on the next page.

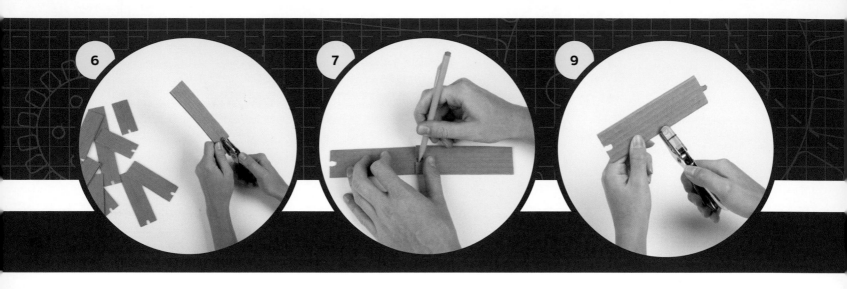

HIGHWAY DESIGN PUZZLE BOARD (CONTINUED)

6 Use the hole punch to make a **notch** at one end of each piece.

7 Lay a notched end of one piece over a straight end of another piece. Trace the notch onto the straight end. Repeat until each piece has a notch traced on its straight end.

8 Cut the traced notches into bumps. Start by cutting in from each side. Then cut around the traced notch.

9 Use the hole punch to make notches in the sides of five of the strips.

10 Draw four curved road pieces on cardboard. Make them 1½ inches (4 cm) wide.

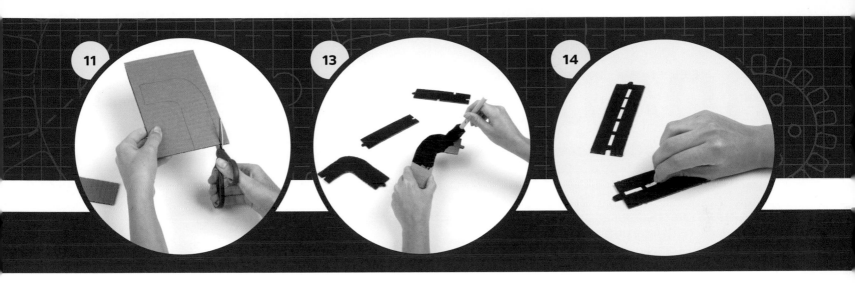

11 Cut out the curved road pieces.

12 Follow step 6 to make a **notch** in one end of each curved piece. Follow steps 7 and 8 to cut a bump in the other end of each curved piece.

13 Paint all of the road pieces black. Let the paint dry.

14 Use correction tape to add a lane dividing line on one side of each piece.

15 Set up **obstacles** on your workspace. Use your road puzzle pieces to build roads around the obstacles. Take the roads apart and start over. How many road systems can you create?

ROAD FORM

MATERIALS: thick cardboard, marker, cutting mat, craft knife, duct tape, craft sticks, scissors, air-dry clay, paint, paintbrush, craft foam

Builders use special molds called forms to shape roads. The forms are built on top of the roadbed. Workers pour concrete into the forms and smooth it out. When the concrete is dry, the workers remove the forms.

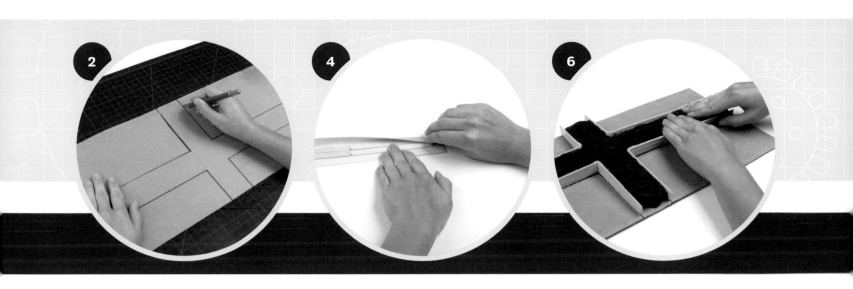

① Draw one or more roads on cardboard.

② Carefully use the craft knife to cut **slits** along the lines. Do not cut all the way through the cardboard.

③ Cut pieces of duct tape the length of each line in your road. Lay the pieces down with the sticky sides up.

④ Lay two rows of craft sticks on a piece of duct tape. Make sure the sticks go the entire length of the tape. Cut the craft sticks shorter if necessary. Fold the tape over the sticks.

⑤ Repeat step 4 with the other pieces of tape. These are the sides of the mold.

⑥ Create the mold by wedging each side into its slit. Then press black clay into the mold. Fill the mold to the top.

⑦ Let the clay dry. Remove the mold. Paint on lane dividing lines.

⑧ Fill in the space around your road. Add layers of dirt and grass using different colors of craft foam.

ROUNDABOUT
SPIN ART DESIGN

MATERIALS: paper plate, scissors, paper cup, marker, ruler, craft knife, duct tape, paper fastener, 2 or 3 pony beads, cardboard box, paint

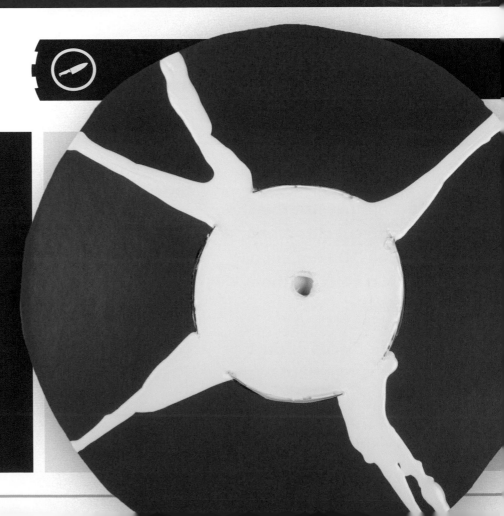

Some road **intersections** have roundabouts. These are also called **traffic** circles. Instead of turning left or right or going straight through, traffic moves in a circle. Roundabouts are more common in Europe than in the United States. But more have been built in the United States since the 1990s.

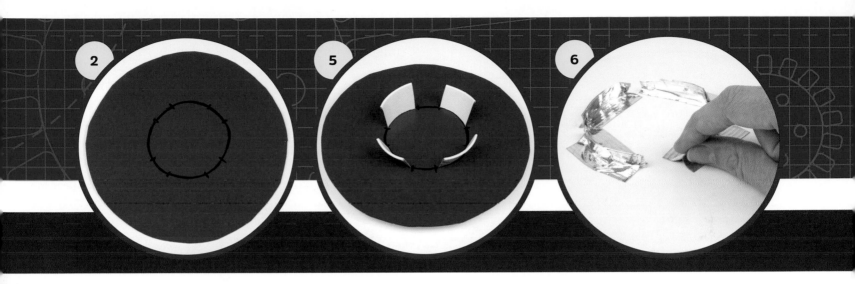

① Cut the rim off of the paper plate. Place the paper cup upside down in the center of the paper plate. Trace around it.

② Mark four ¾-inch (2 cm) sections along the circle. Space them evenly.

③ Use a craft knife to carefully cut **slits** along the circle between the marked sections.

④ Cut the top 1 inch (2.5 cm) off of the paper cup. Cut this ring into pieces that match the slits cut into the plate.

⑤ Push a piece of the cup ring partway through each slit.

⑥ Turn the plate over. Place duct tape over the edges of the cup pieces to hold them in place. This is your roundabout!

Continued on the next page.

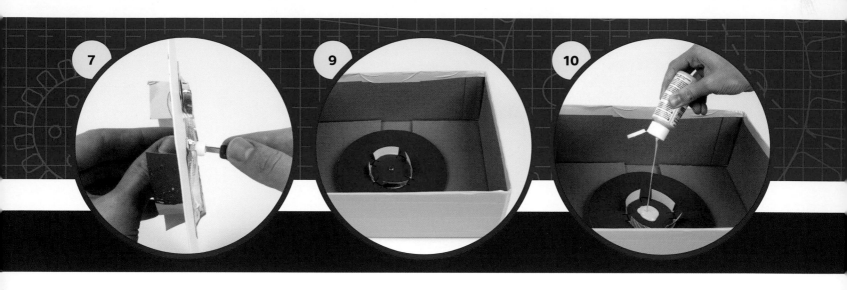

ROUNDABOUT SPIN ART DESIGN (CONTINUED)

⑦ Carefully cut a hole in the center of the roundabout with the craft knife. Push the paper fastener through the hole from top to bottom. Put two or three beads on the end of the fastener.

⑧ Cut the top flaps off of the box. Cover outside of the box with duct tape.

⑨ Cut a small hole in the bottom of the box. Place your roundabout in the box. Stick the paper fastener through the hole in the bottom of the box. Fold the **prongs** of the fastener back. Tape them to the bottom of the box.

⑩ Pour paint into the center of your roundabout.

⑪ Spin the roundabout as fast as you can. Watch the paint move across the roundabout and out the exits!

⑫ Let the paint dry. Remove the walls from your roundabout to reveal the roundabout **design**.

DIGGING DEEPER

A roundabout takes the place of stop signs or stoplights at an **intersection**. A car can enter the circle whenever no cars in the circle are in the way. This means that cars don't have to stop as long before continuing. The result is that cars use less fuel and release less harmful gases into the air. Another result is that drivers get where they are going more quickly. So, roundabouts are good for drivers and the Earth!

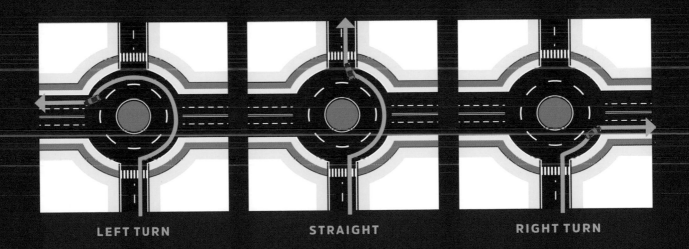

LEFT TURN　　　　STRAIGHT　　　　RIGHT TURN

INERTIA
CHALLENGE

Roads are made for travel. Whether people are walking, driving, or biking on roads, they are moving. And anything that moves is affected by inertia. Inertia means that a moving object will continue at the same speed unless something stops it.

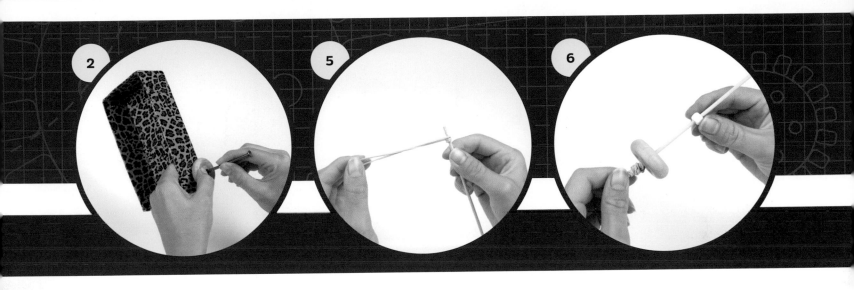

① Cover the entire box with duct tape.

② Hold a wheel so the hole is near the bottom of the box. Make sure part of the wheel hangs down beyond the bottom edge of the box. Push the nail through the wheel hole and the box.

③ Repeat step 2 on the opposite side of the box. Make sure these two holes are directly across from each other.

④ Repeat steps 2 and 3 on the other end of the box.

⑤ Wrap a rubber band around one end of a skewer.

⑥ Put a wheel on the skewer. Add a bead after the wheel.

Continued on the next page.

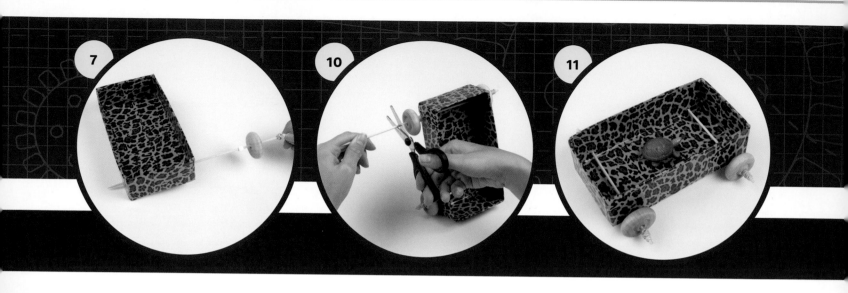

INERTIA CHALLENGE (CONTINUED)

⑦ Push the skewer through both holes on one end of the box.

⑧ Place a bead on the other end of the skewer. Add a wheel. Wrap a rubber band around the skewer near the wheel.

⑨ Repeat steps 5 through 8 to add wheels to the other end of the box.

⑩ Cut the extra length of the skewers off near the rubber bands.

⑪ Place the toy animal in your car.

⑫ Roll the car across a table or the floor. Make it stop suddenly. What happened to the toy?

⑬ Move the car gently and roll it to a smooth stop. What happened to the toy this time?

DIGGING DEEPER

Have you ever been in a car that stopped suddenly? Did you feel your seat belt press across your body? This is inertia at work! You were moving with the car. Then the car stopped and inertia caused you to keep moving until the seat belt stopped you.

Inertia also causes you to move sideways when a car goes around a curve. Engineers **design** roads to reduce the effect of inertia on people in cars. This means curves, turns, and stops must be as safe and gentle as possible.

THE CAR AND PERSON ARE MOVING AT THE SAME SPEED

THE CAR STOPS, BUT THE PERSON KEEPS MOVING FORWARD

THE SEAT BELT STOPS THE PERSON'S FORWARD MOVEMENT

CONCLUSION

Roads are important structures. They let us get around quickly and easily. Roads also help move goods all across the country. But roads require a lot of planning and upkeep. Engineers work hard to build better, safer roads.

QUIZ

1. Which people built the first large road system?

2. When building a road, what **substance** is applied while hot?

3. Route 66 was formed in 1826. **TRUE OR FALSE?**

LEARN MORE ABOUT IT!

You can find out more about roads all over the world at the library. Or you can ask an adult to help you **research** roads **online**.

Answers: 1. The Romans 2. Asphalt 3. False

GLOSSARY

bitumen – a light brown to black solid or semisolid substance. It occurs naturally as asphalt and as a thick crude oil.

crumb – a tiny piece of something, especially food.

design – 1. to plan how something will appear or work. 2. the appearance or style of something.

ditch – a long, narrow hole.

drainage – the drawing or running off of water.

Incas – the people living in the Inca Empire. The Inca Empire existed on the west coast of South America from 1438 to 1533.

intersect – to meet and cross at a point. An intersection is a place where two lines or roads meet each other.

notch – a small, round cut or gap.

obstacle – something that you have to go over or around.

online – connected to the Internet.

prong – one of the sharp points of a fork or tool.

research – to find out more about something.

slit – a narrow cut or opening.

substance – anything that takes up space, such as a solid object or a liquid.

traffic – the cars, trucks, pedestrians, ships, or planes moving along a route.